FIFTY REASONS

Copernicus or the Bible

F. E. Pasche

Fifty Reasons: Copernicus or the Bible

Published by Theonomos (The views expressed in this book are not necessarily the views of the publisher.)

First published in 1915 by F. E. Pasche

ISBN 978-0-9861305-5-7

Fifty Reasons
COPERNICUS OR THE BIBLE

Philosophy and vain deceit or true science? Which is right? ¶ The Bible and Practical Astronomy or the Babel of theoretical, poetical, Newtonian fiction?   :-:   :-:   :-:   :-:

Price 20 Cents

Here are fifty reasons for believing the Bible by
F. E. PASCHE   1915   MORRIS, MINN.

Fifty Reasons

COPERNICUS OR THE BIBLE.

Philosophy and vain deceit or true science? Which is right?

The Bible and Practical Astronomy or the Babel of theoretical, poetical, Newtonian fiction?

"When the Christian layman in Geology or Astronomy finds a discrepancy between the Scriptures and what confronts him as a result of scientific work, the proper thing for him to do is to abide by the Scripture and lay that thing of science aside as erroneous."
Dr. A. L. Graebner, "Quarterly" VI, 42.

Here are fifty reasons for believing the Bible
By F. E. PASCHE, Morris, Minn.
1915

FOREWORD

The author of this booklet has risked a tilt with Science. That is a venturesome undertaking in these days of ours where Science reigns supreme, a veritable goddess before whom millions of faithful worshippers bow their heads in childlike trust. Science has become the masterword to conjure with because it claims to have laid down a firm foundation for a *Weltanschauung* which happily eliminates all those troublous concepts of sin and guilt, of eternity and a responsibility to an almighty God. Whoever dares to touch this beloved and admired idol with an unfriendly hand, with the nefarious purpose of exhibiting its brazen worthlessness, must expect to be caught up in the vortex of a crushing whirlwind of fanatical vituperation. For Science with its highpriests and devotees is intolerant to the last degree.

But let it be remembered that our author is at odds only with Science; he has no quarrel with *science* which is content with a lower-case initial. Just plain science is a valuable aid to man since it diligently assembles knowable facts and marshals them into some logical order for purposes of study and application. Its domain is that of observation, and it rests content with recording what it actually sees and hears. It goes no farther beyond the individual perceptions than to express in general, abstract terms a summary of known facts announcing the so-called "laws" which may be deduced from observed occurrences. Plain science is continuously reaching forward into the region of the unknown, seeking to increase the actual store of human knowledge; but as it never pretends to know what is unknown, so does it never attempt to overstep the boundaries which are set between that which is knowable and that which is naturally unknowable. Briefly, just plain science is real knowledge, not fancy.

But Science, the fetish of the modern world, reincarnation of the ancient idol Philosophy, scorns the boundaries which will forever mark the limit of plain science. From some bare foothold in fact, Science vaults into the saddle of that spirited steed Imagination and sets out to uncover the veiled mysteries of the universe. This adventure would be more promising if the steed were of pure pedigree. But no highpriest of Science could ever command the services of an undefiled imagination; the steed is alway a sideling jade, variously afflicted with pantheism, materialism, evolutionism, atheism, or a combination of these ailments. Thus every foray is doomed to failure at the outset. This fact, though sufficiently vexatious in all conscience, would not necessarily discredit those attempts at reaching the unattainable, if it were generally understood that the fanciful flights of Science were meant for pastime only. But it is an unfortunate habit of Science to proclaim as facts the alleged discoveries made in the trackless realms of fancy. Oh yes, Science will always tell us that this and that is an hypothesis; but Scientists and their unthinking followers, quickly losing sight of the difference between the finest hypothesis and the most insignificant fact, will just as surely insist, after a little while, that what entered the world as a guess becomes a fact by many repetitions. To mention but one instance. The hypothesis of evolutionism, having been adopted by Scientists generally, is not only used as a fact, but insisted upon as such, though to this day no investigator has been able to observe a single case of actual evolution. Hence plain science is compelled to record habitual untruthfulness as one of the deplorable characteristics of Science.

While plain science is not, and never can become, dangerous to a Christian believer, Science has been determinedly at work to overthrow the foundations of faith, and has succeeded in deceiving thousands to their eternal detriment. An accomplishment of which Science is especially proud is the successful destruction of faith in the Scriptures as the real revelation of God. Disguised as astronomy and geology, Science has demonstrated triumphantly that the very first chapters of the Bible contain nothing but myths, which are of no greater historical value than the cosmogony of any pagan people. This was the inevitable result of scientific speculation. No mind imbued with the errors of pantheism, deism, or monism, could by any possibility reconstruct the history of creation along the lines laid down in the record of which God is the author. It matters not that all the real *facts* of astronomy and geology agree very well with the Mosaic presentation and the point of view prevailing in the whole Bible; since Science has decreed that these facts shall be utilized for deductions based upon other points of view, and has declared its deductions to be facts, thousands of deluded sinners have been led to discard as antiquated the entire revelation of God in the Bible, including the Savior and His salvation.

Thus, since Science (not plain science, mind you!) is at war with the fundamental doctrines of Christian faith, it follows that all true Christians must be at war with Science. They cannot sit complacently by while the vain imaginings of the princes of this world are offered as true answers to the most vital questions with which every human being is concerned. It is in this spirit that our author makes his attack upon Science. Sure of his foothold in the inerrant Word of God, he, in particular, aims to show up the fatal weakness of the vaunted deductions of Astronomy (not astronomy, please!). The reader may not agree with the writer in every argument. He may, for instance, admit the possibility that the statements of Scripture referring to the sun as a moving body, were not meant to say that the sun does really move (though such an admission is much like playing with fire!). But he will surely agree that the writer has successfully arraigned Science for untruthfulness in allowing the impression to prevail that its astronomical hypotheses have attained the dignity of facts, whereas they can never be established as such. If it is too much to hope that this brief treatise will actually bring back some erring hearts to certain faith in the Bible, it will surely be welcomed as a fearless witness of the truth by those who, though certain of their footing in Holy Scripture, are yet conscious of the unholy power of Science to corrupt the heart of a believer.

Wauwatosa, Wis., March 27, 1915.

J. SCHALLER.

CONTENTS

		PAGE
1.	The *earth* stands fast	1
2.	The pendulum experiment	1
3.	Job 26, 7	3
4.	Our atmosphere	3
5.	The Trade Winds	4
6.	A law of nature?	5
7.	Ocean currents	5
8.	Contradicting the hypothesis	6
9.	Earth, the central body	6
10.	Gravitation against rotation	7
11.	The flattened poles	7
12.	Falling bodies	8
13.	Richer's discovery	9
14.	The *sun* moves	10
15.	What does "*shemesh*" mean?	11
16.	Zodiacal light	11
17.	Earth older than sun	12
18.	Waters above firmament	12
19.	Biblical plan more rational	13
20.	The vapors of water	14
21.	Scientists baffled	16
22.	Conservation of energy	16
23.	Agrees with chemistry	17
24.	Copernican difficulties	18
25.	Comets against them	19
26.	Orbit around the sun	20
27.	An impossibility	21
28.	Sun through space	22
29.	Attraction and repulsion	23
30.	Results of theory erroneous	24
31.	Fundamentally false	24
32.	Elliptical orbits crushed	24
33.	Against nature of earth	26
34.	Motion natural for sun	26
35.	Very plausible	26
36.	Parallax of stars	26
37.	Roemer's discovery	27
38.	Bradley's observation	28
39.	Spectroscope favors Bible	30
40.	Biblical view explains more	30
41.	They minister to the earth	31
42.	Bible implies reality	32
43.	Ps. 74, 16; Eccl. 1, 4. 5	33
44.	No insignificant things	35
45.	No erroneous conceptions of men	35
46.	Only one, the literal sense	36
47.	We must accept literal meaning	37
48.	Appearance ("*Optice*")	39
49.	Full conviction	41
50.	Theory and superstition	43

> "*I consider thy heavens, the work of thy fingers, the moon and the stars, which thou hast ordained.*"
>
> Psalm 8, 3.

FIFTY REASONS.

1. According to the Bible, *the earth stands still in space*. Psalm 93, 1: "The earth stands fast that it cannot be moved." I Chronicles 16, 30: "The world also shall be stable, that it be not moved." Psalm 104, 5: "He hath founded the earth upon its base, that it should not be removed forever." As a builder constructs a house on a base or a foundation that it stands firm against the storm, even so has the heavenly architect firmly founded the earth, this great building, upon its base, so that it can never be moved from its place. Psalm 119, 90: "Thou hast established the earth, and it standeth." These are only a few passages out of many. It is the literal truth of the Bible. And Jesus, our Redeemer, endorses it by saying: "And the Scripture cannot be broken." (John 10, 35.) And through his apostle he states: "All Scripture is given by inspiration of God, and is profitable for doctrine." (2 Tim. 3, 16.) Should we not, then, accept the above passages as divine truth?

2. But did not *Foucault's pendulum* prove that the earth revolves in twenty-four hours upon its axis? In the introduction to Ray's Elements of Astronomy Mr. Peabody calls it "a beautiful experiment." Andrew White triumphantly exclaims: "And in 1851 the great experiment of Foucault with the pendulum showed to the human eye the earth in motion around its own axis." (Warfare, 1900, I, p. 157.) Let us glance briefly at the instrument called the pendulum. Foucault's pendulum had a sixty-one pound ball on a steel-wire 223 feet in length. If we let a pendulum occillate in a direction north and south, then will its even oscillation, as Foucault assumes, be unaffected by the rotation of the plane, and consequently the earth will move ahead below its swinging-line. Now, if this is to prove the rotation of the earth, the deviation of the earth below from the swinging-line of the pendulum must be in all cases the same. But the trouble is, the deviation is not the same with all pendulums. The heavier the bob, the slower becomes the deviation of

the pendulum; the lighter the bob, the more rapidly the deviation. Since the rotation of the earth upon its axis, if existing, must be a uniform one, necessarily with all pendulums the deviation should be uniform; but this is not the case. Or does the earth move with different velocity under different pendulums? Dr. Schoepffer, an eye-witness of the experiment, says: "In an introductory speech Dr. Menzzer at Quedlinburg showed that until then there had been no proof for the Copernican hypothesis, the so-called proofs being, after close investigation, just as many confutations, until the Foucault pendulum showed the rotation of the earth uncontrovertibly. The pendulum was tied, the string was burnt, the swingings began, but the pendulum deviated to the left, instead of to the right. It was hastily brought to rest. New burning of the string. This time the deviation was the one desired, and we were invited again to be present in the church the next morning at eight o'clock, to be convinced that the deviation agrees with the theory. On the following morning, however, we saw that the pendulum during the night had changed its mind, and had from the deviation to the right again returned to the left. To me this new proof did not seem to be quite in order. My belief in the Copernican doctrine was shaken by the speech of Dr. Menzzer, and I concluded to go to Berlin for an explanation. After seeing the pendulum-experiment here also and, strangely, again with a deviation to the left, I went to Alexander v. Humboldt, who was indeed ever the first refuge of those seeking information. He received me very friendly and spoke the memorable words: I have known, too, for a long time, that as yet we have no proof for the Copernican system, but I shall never dare to be the first to attack it. Don't rush into the wasps' nest. You will but bring upon yourself the scorn of the thoughtless multitude." Furthermore, I have found, by careful experiments, that a skillful experimenter can let the pendulum deviate either to the left or to the right. And we must not overlook the fact that the deviations may be caused by air-currents, electricity, earth-magnetism, special apparatus, and perhaps many other causes. Blunt and Cox observed the most curious and contrary swingings. Phillips of New York found very great hourly deviations in the swinging-line. Walker observed a peculiarly swift deviation when the pendulum swings in the magnetic meridian. D'Oliveira at Rio de Janeiro stated that the pendulum deviates to the right in the direction of the meridian, but to the left in the direction of the parallel. This deviation, diametrically opposed to the theory, was seen very often. And sometimes the pendulum does not deviate at all. Much more could be said against this "beautiful experiment." Though beautiful it may seem to the theorist, it certainly is far from being irrefragable evidence for the earth's motion.

3. But how is it possible that the ponderous earth can stand still hanging on nothing, some Copernican will exclaim. Yet just that is the case; for we read Job 26, 7: "He stretcheth out the north over the empty place, and *hangeth the earth upon nothing."* To this Matthew Henry remarks in his commentary: "The vast terraqueous globe neither rests upon any pillars, nor hangs upon any axle-tree; and yet, by the almighty power of God, is firmly fixed in its place, poised with its own weight. The art of man could not hang a feather upon nothing, yet the Divine Wisdom hangs the whole earth so. It is *ponderibus librata suis*—poised by its own weight, so says the poet; it is upheld by the word of God's power, so says the apostle." The Bible denies a motion of the earth. Ecclesiastes 1, 4: "The earth abideth (Hebrew: *amad*=stands, rests) forever."

4. Further incontestable proof for the fact that the earth stands fast is *our atmosphere*. The air which surrounds us, always tends to expand. We have proof for an immense height of the air. When Humboldt stood on Mount Chimborasso in Ecuador, South America, that mountain being 20,648 feet or nearly four miles high, he saw a condor soaring far above him like a little speck. Scientists tell us that the atmosphere or aeriform fluid surrounding the earth is about fifty miles high. We are told that under the equator everything moves eastward with a speed of 1,250 feet in a second because the earth rotates. Were it possible that the ever expansive air should be able to follow such speedy motion? Assuredly not; it would be retarded and seem to rush westward 1,250 feet in a second, which would more than ten times surpass the velocity of the most fearful hurricane. Add to this a motion of the earth around the sun and another of the sun through space, and you have the astounding speed of fifty miles in a second! Must not by this the air be entirely lost, or at least follow the earth like the tail of a comet? Copernicans tell us that just by the rapid motion the air is pressed tight to the

earth. But can they show us where the pressure begins or takes place? We certainly ought to feel or notice something of a pressure so fabulous and enormous. However, we feel it not in the least. We see the smoke rise free and unmolested up into the air, calmly the clouds sail to and fro far over us, the air-ship rises and ascends above the clouds: but nowhere is the swift motion of the earth or that mysterious pressure felt. Where, then, is it?

5. Our opponents have felt that argument. They clearly saw that the great pressure caused by the earth's rotation ought to be noticed somehow. For that reason they have always urged that the *Trade Winds* in the hot belt are caused by the swiftly moving earth. While the earth moves eastwardly, the Trade Winds move westwardly. However, not only are these winds much too unstable to prove the earth's steady motion, but this theory is also thoroughly refuted by other air-currents, quite regularly moving eastwardly, in direct contrast to the theory. Now, after accurate meteorological observations of more than sixty years it is generally known that, as a rule, the winds in the temperate zone do not move westwardly like the Trade Winds, but eastwardly. In the cold zone however they move, as a rule, toward south-east. Therefore Prof. Joseph Henry of our Meteorological Institution at Washington carefully called this proof of the Copernicans a mere hypothesis and admitted: "The effects produced by the air, the water, and the land, are however of a much more complicated character, and like the problem of the mutual action of all the planets on each other, have never yet been submitted to a successful mathematical analysis." (Scientific Writings, II, 44f.) As early as March 11, 1861, the director of the Smithsonian Institution wrote to an air-ship sailor by the name of Lowe: "It has been fully established by continuous observations for ten years collected at this Institution from every part of the United States, that as a general rule all the meteorological phenomena advance from west to east, and that the higher clouds always move eastwardly." But that is directly opposed to the theory. It is high time for Copernicans to learn that the direction of the winds is not referable to the rotation of the earth upon its axis in the sense of receiving its impetus from that motion. In our scientific and enlightened age it ought to be known that change of atmosphere, temperature, cloud-formation, rainfall, direction of the winds, and other

weather phenomena and meteorological elements, are dependent principally upon the influence of sun and moon.

6. If the Foucault pendulum is not disturbed by the earth's rotation, *how, then, is it that the atmosphere must obediently follow that motion?* May we not deduct from the "beautiful" pendulum-experiment, that an eagle soaring up in New York must after two hours come down in California, having, together with the surrounding air, been undisturbed by the rapidly moving earth? Or, if that dreamed of great pressure of our atmosphere really existed, must not a balloon in which the air is extremely extenuated, crush together in consequence of such pressure and tendency of the surrounding air? Is it not, after all, the most natural thing that, because of its great expansibility, the air should press, not downward, but upward into open space? We cannot put a limit to the atmosphere above us. We must accept it as a fact that *the whole space around us is filled with air.* It is a well-known property of the air to fill all empty space. The air possesses a tendency toward expansion. As to hydrogen the Copernicans themselves must admit, against their theory, that the earth cannot hold its hydrogen. It is produced abundantly on the earth, but does not remain here. Where does it stay? It escapes into space. And this seems very natural, since, according to modern science, a material medium called *ether,* a fine elastic substance, fills all space. Why not, then, call it by *one* name and say, *our atmosphere* extends into all surrounding space connecting the earth with sun, moon, and stars, and being the carrier of light and electricity. True, this does not agree with the embraced theory, but it agrees very well with science and the Bible.

7. Further, Copernicans say that *ocean-currents* demonstrate a diurnal rotation of the earth. But to be consistent with the theory *all* the currents should move westwardly. But this is far from being the case, it being the notorious fact that they move in every possible direction. The true causes of the ocean-currents are summed up by Prof. Henry, that learned scientist, thus: "Heated water is constantly carried from the equatorial regions towards the poles, and streams of cold water returned . . . The continued action of the wind on the surface of the water would evidently give rise to a current of the ocean in the belt over which the wind passed. The regularity of their outline will be disturbed by the configuration of the deflecting

coasts and the form of the bottom of the sea, as well as by islands, irregular winds, difference of temperature, and above all, by the annual motion of the sun as it changes its declination." (Joseph Henry, Scientific Writings, II, 14. 61.) When a Copernican writer in the Tivoli Times, September 7, 1900, held that the "mysterious power" of the *earth's rotation* deflects the Gulf Stream, General J. Watts de Peyster, after clearly showing the fallacy of the argument, correctly added: "To say the least, the attempt to introduce an effect of the earth's rotation here, as an additional agency of the same kind, is entirely superfluous. But if the earth rotates, there *should* be such an effect; so that the failure to perceive it is an argument against the Copernican theory." Also this difficulty falls down the moment the immagined rotation of the earth is discarded. One of the strong arguments advanced by Dr. Schoepffer in his excellent book "The Earth Stands Fast" (Berlin, 1869) against the rotation theory is that such a movement should produce both air-currents and ocean-currents of a powerful and decided type, such as do not, in fact, exist!

8. *The forms of our continents contradict the hypothesis of the rotation of the earth.* Were there such a rotation, these formations would have been built up in the main directions, from east to west; whereas, in reality, we find their longitudinal development from north to south. This argument is greatly strengthened by the modern theory of tidal friction, which has led physicists to the conclusion that during its early formative period the earth performed its axial rotation in two hours! Is it not strange that the trend of continents should be so absolutely opposed to the cherished theory? Ponder this fact.

9. That there are no fixed stars proper has been demonstrated by the peculiar orbital motions which those fixed stars have in addition to their daily course about the earth. The astronomers have therefore sought in vain for *a central body,* the attraction of which would keep those stars in their course. But there must be such a central body, and *it must be our earth.* This was also the conclusion attained, after the most profound and comprehensive investigation of this problem, by Dr. Alfred Russel Wallace, a man of acknowledged scientific ability. A time ago, in The Fortnightly Review, this learned author and much honored scientist told a startled world

that the solar system is the centre of the universe, that the earth is the only inhabited globe, and that the entire creation was ordered and designed for man's sole benefit and accommodation. And corresponding to the greater formation of land upon the northern hemisphere, the greater number of stars is found on the northern half of the heavens.

10. "Newton announced to the world the great law of universal gravitation." (Emma Willard, Astronomy.) Which is this 'great' law? Newton said, "The centres of all bodies are attracted towards each other, directly as the quantity of matter, and inversely as the square of their distance." Dr. Schoepffer, General de Peyster, and Frank Allaben are absolutely correct in saying that this *Newtonian gravitation,* if consistent with the other laws of nature, *would prevent the axial rotation* of any body which by gravity is maintained in equilibrium in an orbit of revolution about an attractive centre, with the exception of a single rotation during the orbital revolution. Thus we know of the moon which is nearest to us, that she actually does not rotate, but always shows us the same familiar face. Tack a string to a ball, hold the other end of the string in the fingers, and swing the ball in a circle with sufficient velocity to keep the string taut: here you have the resolution of attractive pull and centrifugal tendency known to nature. Because the attracting pull is constant, throughout its orbit of revolution, the ball ever keeps one and the same face to the attracting power. This is what we find in the case of the moon, whose attracting centre is the earth. This argument is now notably emphasized by the conclusion of Schiaparelli, Lowell and others, attesting the like phenomena in the orbital revolutions of Mercury and Venus about the sun. Thus if the moon, Venus and Mercury conform in this particular to the theory that all the atoms of each are attracted by all the atoms of sun and earth, then it is certain that the axial rotation of the earth is in direct violation to the ruling Newtonian theory. Really, this Newtonian dream of gravitation is a "great" law!

11. Already Newton pointed out that in virtue of the daily rotation, the earth must be *flattened at the poles.* Evolutionary astronomers tell us this flattening at the poles took place when the earth's crust was cooling in an early period of its formation. In his book on astronomy p. 76 Prof. Ball, the great Copernican, calls this

"a remarkable confirmation" of the earth's rotation. And it really is very remarkable that the flattening at the poles should be *caused* by the rotation of the earth; for this is not the case with other bodies, as for instance the sun. The sun too rotates we are told. But Prof. Ball tells us p. 185: "The most careful observations have not afforded reliable indications of any elipticity in the figure of the sun." According to the theory, however, the earth must be flattened at the poles. And measuring the meridians of the earth, it was found by some that they are longer toward the poles, although the measurements made on various occasions do not in the least agree. Writes Sir Norman Lockyer: "The polar diameter is 41,709,790 feet; but the equator is not a circle, the equatorial diameter from longitude 8° 15' west to longitude 188° 15' west is 41,853,258 feet; that at right angles to it is 41,850,210 feet; that is, some thousand yards shorter. The earth, then, is shaped like an orange slightly squeezed." (New York Sun, 1901.) According to Ray, Elements of Astronomy, p. 78 one earth-diameter at the equator is 8,968 feet, or about $1\frac{3}{5}$ miles shorter than another. Thus *the measurements of the degrees have failed to prove the rotation of the earth.* And may not the larger degrees near the poles, if they really exist, be due to a *lengthened* pole, and the earth have the shape of a lemon? We have here another alleged proof of the rotation of the earth which I cannot accept, and which has been repudiated by others before me.

12. As early as 1679 Newton advanced the idea that bodies falling from a high steeple would in virtue of the earth's rotation fall somewhat east of the straight line downward. In the steeple of St. Michael's Church at Hamburg, Benzenberg in 1804 dropped thirty balls from a height of 235 feet and reaped much applause in the "scientific" circles. And Andrew White triumphantly brings the old story in his renowned "Warfare," vol. I., stating: "Benzenburg has experimentally demonstrated just such an aberration in *falling bodies* as is mathematically required by the diurnal motion of the earth." But which are the facts? Those thirty balls fell toward every cardinal point, so that all possible deductions could de drawn from that experiment. Benzenberg himself stated that a draught of the air in the steeple caused the failure. This, then, explains the general silence about the experiment, when recently that church burnt down. What, then, has Benzenberg "demonstrated"? This:

we cannot perceive the rotation of the earth in any way. We cannot demonstrate it! Or was that draught of air in the steeple due to the earth swiftly rotating? There are no air-currents which we can justly regard as consequences of such rotation. These facts ought to be proof enough against the existence of a rotation of the earth.— More recently experiments are said to have been made in the shafts of the copper mines at Calumet, Michigan. But in the first place it must be said that these shafts or entrances to the mines are much too narrow for such experiments, and further, that, to be convincing, such experiments must be made at many other places, because the deviation of the metallic balls may be caused by minerals, earth-magnetism, and last not least (like Benzenberg's draught of air in the Hamburg steeple) by—a *draught* in the shaft!

13. We now go on to the last consideration by means of which the rotation of the earth is thought to be demonstrated. We read in the Encyclopedia Britannica: "The motion of the earth can, indeed, never be made an object of ocular demonstration, but after Richer's discovery of the *diminuation of gravity towards the equator,* it was impossible to doubt longer of the existence of its rotary motion." It is this. The Frenchman Richer observed in the year 1672 that a pendulum clock going normally in Paris lost daily two and one-half minutes in Cayenne, five degrees north of the equator, and he had to shorten the pendulum by one-eighth of an inch to make it go correctly. Therefore, it was argued, the gravity or attraction under the equator must be less, since the pendulum there makes slower oscillations; and it was concluded that the centrifugal tendency caused by the motion of the earth upon its axis reduced the gravity, and consequently made the movement of the pendulum slower. But this conclusion again lacks infallibility, for we may just as well suppose that the attraction of the earth diminishes with the distance from its centre, which is at the same time the centre of attraction. The earth's diameter at the equator is, as the Copernicans themselves say, 26 miles longer than the diameter at the pole. According to this we are at the equator thirteen miles farther away from the centre of the earth, and hence the decreased attraction and the slackening of the oscillations of the pendulum in the middle latitudes and upon high mountains. Further, it is a fact—which seems to be unknown to many philosophers, although most of the old village schoolmasters

were aware of it—that the quicker or slower movements of the pendulum do not depend exclusively upon its length, but also upon the weight of the bob. Hence we may obtain the same result by increasing the weight of the bob, instead of lengthening the rod of the pendulum. The larger the weight of the bob, the slower the oscillations of the pendulum. The deductions from these observations, carried out by Laugier with the utmost care, are as follows: (a) The laws of Galileo in regard to the oscillations of the pendulum are not exactly correct; (b) the decrease of the attraction of the earth toward the equator, inferred from the decrease of the velocity of the pendulum, is probably wrong; (c) the laws of falling bodies, so far universally accepted, are also probably not exact; (d) calculations of physical laws in general are always untrustworthy, as only experience can decide. (Published in the "Comptes Rendus de l'Academie Francaise," vol. XXI, pp. 117-124.) Indeed we wholly lack a consideration indicating rotation which can be substantiated. Must it not appear almost absurd that we, preoccupied, as we are, by what they have taught us in school, should accept a theory of the rotation of the earth which neither is, nor can be, proven? Must we not wonder at the readiness of the learned of nearly the entire world, from the time of Copernicus and Kepler, to accept the conception of the rotation of the earth—and then search afterwards, now for nearly four centuries, for arguments to maintain it, but of course without being able to find them?

14. While the Copernican hypothesis refers the daily revolution of the celestial bodies to a rotation of the earth, the Bible refers that daily revolution to the celestial bodies rather than to the earth. *The Scriptures everywhere and consistently ascribe the daily motion to the sun, moon, and stars.* Isaiah 40, 26: "Lift up your eyes on high, and behold who hath created these things, that *bringeth out their host* by number: he calleth them all by names by the greatness of his might, for that he is strong in power; not one faileth." Psalm 148, 3. 6: "Praise ye him, sun and moon: praise him, all ye stars of light. He upholds them forever and ever: he hath made a decree which they shall not trespass." They always accurately keep their prescribed course. Ecclesiastes 1, 5: "The sun also ariseth, and the sun goeth down, and hasteth (margin: panteth) to his place where he arose."

15. The sun moves in a spiral line, or winding like a screw, around the earth, southward from June till December and northward from December till June. He therefore daily stays behind the stars about four minutes, thus marching through all the stars within a year. *The Hebrew word for sun* is *shemesh,* and he is called thus because of his swift motion. The verb shamash means to run hastily, to move very fast. Now, since all Scripture is given by inspiration of God and "holy men of God spake as they were moved by the Holy Ghost" (2 Pet. 1, 21), since even the single words were inspired by God, 1 Cor. 2, 13: "Which things also we speak not in the *words* which man's wisdom teacheth, but which the Holy Ghost teacheth," must not the Creator Himself be Anti-Copernican? He undoubtedly is. Then, ponder this fact!

16. *The zodiacal light is in favor of the sun's daily motion.* The cause and nature of the zodiacal light have never been explained in a satisfactory way by Newtonian-Copernican astronomers, although this is one of the puzzles to which ingenious investigators have addressed themselves since the days of Kepler. The zodiacal light has the appearance of a huge, faintly luminous cloud of matter, which attends the sun in his daily circuit of the earth. After sundown it appears in the western sky, the point where the sun has disappeared behind the horizon being the centre of its base, from which it slants to an apex often extending upward for ninety degrees. Our American astronomers Newcomb and Holden confess in their text-book of Astronomy p. 387: "Its origin is still involved in obscurity." Prof. Norton of Yale College writes (Astronomy. Fourth edition, p. 178): "At Quito the light was seen every favorable night, at all hours, to extend as a broad luminous arch, entirely from one horizon to the other." Miss Agnes Clerke, History of Astronomy, fourth edition, p. 177, says: "The peculiar structure at the base of the streamers displayed in the photographs, the curved rays meeting in pointed arches like Gothic windows, the visible upspringing tendency, the filamentous texture, speak *unmistakably* of the action of forces proceeding *from the sun,* not of extraneous matter circling round him." How, then, can the Copernicans account for this fact in nature? They have as yet failed to do so. But the moment we assume as true the Biblical plan of the sun's daily movement round the earth, this difficult problem receives a solution so simple and ob-

vious that it becomes in turn a powerful argument in favor of the Biblical view. Ponder the fact! Remember, that all facts are infallible. If there were but one fact to sustain the Bible statements, there is not one fact to sustain the statements of the Copernican astronomers.

17. That *the earth is older than the sun*, is fully borne out by the first chapter of Genesis. But the theorists maintain that the Copernican system necessitates the assumption of millions of years of siderial existence and excludes the possibility of the creation of the sun and the moon and the stars on the fourth day of the hexaemeron and after the appearance of vegetation on the earth, and that, consequently, the Mosaic record of the creation must be laid aside as untenable. What, then, is the duty of every Christian? Answer: "Every intelligent Christian and every convention of Christians ought to be competent and ready to stand by the truth of the plain words recorded in Genesis against the opposing errors advanced in the name of science." (Graebner, Theol. Quarterly, 1902 p. 42.) The two beliefs—modern science and the Bible cannot possibly be held together in the same mind. He who thinks he believes both, knows little of either.

18. The Copernican plan is an impossibility. Genesis 1, 7. 8: "And God made the firmament and divided the *waters* which were under the firmament from the waters which were *above the firmament*: and it was so. And God called the firmament Heaven." The firmament is the space through which sun, moon, and stars move. This we clearly see from verses 14 and 15: "And God said, Let there be lights *in the firmament* of the heaven to divide the day from the night . . . And let them be for lights *in the firmament* of the heaven to give light upon the earth: and it was so." And a little further it is said of the birds that they fly "in the face of the firmament of heaven" i. e. *under the firmament*. This meaning is substantiated by the whole context. In verse 2 we hear that at first earth and water were mixed. According to verse 6 God on the second day created a firmament between the waters which should "divide the waters from the waters." And according to verse 7 he divided the waters *under* the firmament from the waters *above* the firmament. Then in verse 8 this division is called the firmament of heaven, and in verse 11 we are told that on this division between the

waters below and above, or in other words: into the firmament of heaven, he put the celestial lights. Nothing is clearer than this context. Our meaning is also borne out by other passages. Psalm 148, 3-5: "Praise ye him, sun and moon: praise him, all ye stars of light. Praise him, ye heavens of heavens, and ye *waters that be above the heavens.* Let them praise the name of the Lord: for he commanded, and they were created." Also Psalm 104, 3 those waters are mentioned, but as not the same as the water in the clouds. That the clouds or rain-water cannot be meant, we see from Genesis 2, 5. 6 where we are told that it had not rained before the third day when the plants were made, and now we read: "But there went up a mist from the earth, and watered the whole face of the ground." This shows that it was no fog or rain-water which God put over the firmament on the second day. At the close of the second day it was said: "And it was so." What? The waters were gathered under and above the starry skies; but fog and rain there was not until the third day. But conceded that by the expression "firmament of heaven" the air were meant, even then clouds and rain-water could not be above the firmament, for these are *in* the air, never *above* the air. Genesis 1, 7 however decidedly speaks of the waters *above* the firmament. Again, the firmament is spoken of as a division between the waters below and above so that they cannot come together. But does not the rain come down from the clouds, and are not immense quantities of water continually drawn up into the clouds by evaporation? So much to corroborate the Bible truth that there are vast oceans of water above sun, moon, and stars. And this has always been the position of the better part of the theologians, especially of Luther and the learned Lutheran theologian Dr. Aug. Pfeiffer, also of the late Dr. Stoeckhardt. You see at once that in view of this Biblical astronomical system the Copernican theory becomes an impossibility.

19. But far from being absurd, this Biblical astronomical system explains many problems in astronomy *much more rationally than the Copernican view*. This Biblical system fully solves the puzzling problem of the conservation of energy which has baffled the ablest physicists of our enlightened age. All man's experimental attempts to establish a perpetual transformation of energy have been baffled by the dissipation of energy. The scientist has concluded that the dissi-

pation of energy is a law of the universe, and that in the course of time the great physical clock-work of this world must run down. Scientists have always felt, that, could the Newtonian and Copernican hypothesis help us to formulate a rational conception of how the physical universe might self-subsist indefinitely, this would go far toward demonstrating their truth. Laplace thought he had effected this. But time has demonstrated the failure of Laplace, as well as of his predecessors and successors, as Prof. Hall concedes; while through the lack of such a demonstration physicists have been forced to the other extreme of postulating the principle of the dissipation of energy, involving the ultimate relapse of the universe into passivity and immobility. But when we accept the Biblical system, and conceive the waters above sun, moon, and stars to be the grand reservoir of potential energy which it is constantly giving forth to the swiftly revolving celestial bodies, it becomes perfectly rational to think of the sun and the other luminaries as receiving again all the energy which they dissipate in the process of doing work, and that thus the whole mechanism of the universe is maintained.

20. How can water do that? This is easily demonstrated by the following simple experiment. We pour water into a U shaped tube and let an electric current go through it. At once the water diminishes and little bubbles rise from it to the surface, but at one end of the tube twice as many as at the other end. We now light a match which extinguishes at that end of the tube where there are less bubbles, but flares up into a large flame at the other end where there are twice as many. How is this? By the electric current the water was decomposed into its two elements: 1. into oxygen, and: 2. into hydrogen, an inflammable gas. Of the latter water contains twice as much as of the first. May not, thus, also the waters above the firmament be decomposed into their elements feeding the swiftly moving heavenly bodies? Is not this a very plausible conception, and does not thus the Biblical view become very rational? Lately the scientists come very close to the Biblical view. Dr. Tyndall writes: "Up to the present point, I have omitted all reference to the most important vapor of all, as far as our world is concerned—the *vapor of water*. This vapor is always diffused *through the atmosphere*. The clearest day is not exempt from it: indeed, in the Alps, the purest skies are often the most treacherous, the firmamental

blue deepening with the amount of aqueous vapor in the air. It is needless, therefore, to remind you that when aqueous vapor is spoken of, nothing visible is meant. It is not fog; nor is it cloud or mist of any kind. These are formed of vapor which has been condensed to water; but the true vapor, with which we have to deal, is an impalpable transparent gas. . . *The aqueous vapor which absorbs heat thus greedily, radiates it copiously.* . . Of the *numerous wonderful properties of water,* not the least important is the power which it possesses, of *discharging the motion of heat upon the interstellar ether."* (Heat a Mode of Motion. Sixth Edition. N. Y. 1883 p. 373f.) Then arose the two great standing enigmas of meteorology: What is the color of the sky and the polarization of its light? Says Dr. Tyndall: "But there is still another subject connected with our firmament, of a more subtle and recondite character than even its color. I mean that 'mysterious and beautiful phenomenon' (Herschel's Meteorology, art. 233), the polarization of the light of the sky. Brewster, Arago, Babinet, Herschel, Wheatstone, Rubeson and others, have made us masters of the phenomenon, but its cause remains a mystery still." (p. 485f.) Sir David Brewster: "The more the subject is considered, the more it will be found beset with difficulties." Sir John Herschel: "The reflection would have to be made *in* air *upon* air! Were the angle of maximum polarization 76°, we should look to *water,* or ice, *as the reflecting body,* however inconceivable the existence in a cloudless atmosphere, and a hot summer day, of unevaporated particles of *water."* (p. 489.) Dr. Williams: "As the examination of the sun and stars proceeded, chemists were amazed or delighted, according to their various preconceptions, to witness the proof that many familiar terrestrial elements are to be found in the celestial bodies. But what perhaps surprised them most was to observe the *enormous preponderance in the siderial bodies of the element hydrogen."* (Nineteenth-Century Science, p. 286.) But hydrogen, an inflammable gas, is one of the elements of water. Does it not seem very natural then that this element, drawn from the waters above the firmament, feeds and sustains the heavenly bodies? Not only are there vast quantities of this element in the sun, but also in the other heavenly bodies. "If the sun were a solid mass of coal, he would be totally consumed in about five thousand years. As no such decrease in size as this implies had taken place

...n historic times, it was clear that some other explanation must be sought." (Williams, p. 436f.) The Biblical system fully offers it. Does not therefore the astronomical plan of the Bible seem very natural?

21. The Biblical plan must be the more acceptable, since science, or rather, *the scientist is totally baffled* and confesses: Here we are ignorant. Says C. A. Young: "Time was when there was no such solar heat as now, and the time *must* come when it will cease." (The Sun. Second Edition, p. 275.) Sir William Thomson: "Will the sun, then, keep up for ever a supply of this force? It cannot, if it be not replenished, and at present we are ignorant of any known means." S. H. Parkes: "What material source of supply has science discovered for the replenishing of that enormous waste which must have been going on? Many attempts have been made during the past century, to answer these questions. . . One of the grandest and most complete theories hitherto propounded was one which the late Dr. Siemens brought before the Royal Society." (Unfinished Worlds, p. 61f.) And Dr. Young says: "Dr. C. W. Siemens, of London, has recently proposed a new theory relating to the source and maintenance of the sun's heat, which, on account of the eminence of the author, is exciting much interest and discussion in scientific circles." (The Sun, p. 315.) Which is this theory? The fundamental conditions of Dr. Siemens's theory are the following, in his own words: "1. That aqueous vapor and carbon compounds are present in stellar and interplanetary space. 2. That these 'compounds can be dissociated by radiant solar energy, while in a state of extreme attenuation.' And 3. That these dissociated *vapors are capable of being compressed into the solar atmosphere by* a process of interchange with an equal amount of reassociated vapors, the interchange being effected by the centrifugal *action of the sun itself."* But whence do these vapors come? The Newtonian-Copernican theory knows no answer, while the Biblical system has a very good answer. Should not scientists, then, seriously reconsider the Biblical plan of the universe?

22. Dr. Siemens's theory has been opposed by some scientists because it seemed to them somewhat 'complicated.' But that should be no reason for them to reject it. The learned Prof. E. S. Holden (formerly director of Lick Observatory) answers them as follows:

"Many modern theories are *complex* to a degree, *but this is no proof that they are not true.* . . We in our day have learned a patient tolerance of opinion; wait, these theories that seem so baseless may, perhaps, come to something, as others have done in the past. To what especial and peculiar merit do we owe this acquired virtue of tolerant patience? It is owed solely to the experience of centuries. We have so often seen the impossible become the plausible, and at last the proved and the practical." (Popular Science Monthly, 1904, p. 332f.) Though complex the Biblical record of waters above the firmament and the theory of Dr. Siemens may seem, yet we must accept both as true. Of the latter Dr. C. A. Young in his celebrated book "The Sun," p. 166 has well said: "It may be said in the first place, that there is nothing absurd in it. . . If space is filled with composite vapors, and if rays of light and heat can decompose them again into their elements, then, to some extent, the theory not only *may* be but *must* be true. A hot revolving globe *moving* in a space filled with such vapors, must necessarily produce such currents as Dr. Siemens indicates, and must maintain a continual fire upon its surface." *By the Biblical scheme* of waters above the firmament as reservoirs of energy, the energy of the universe is never diminished and *the great problem and all-important law of the conservation of energy is most satisfactorily solved.* Taking the so-called physical forces in what seems to be a convenient order of transformation, we have a circular chain which returns into itself as follows: heat produces light, light produces chemical action, chemical action produces electricity, electricity produces magnetism, magnetism produces mechanical motion, mechanical motion produces heat. Scientists have puzzled over the postulate of some universal energy behind this circle. Which is it? The Biblical scheme points to the sun himself as "the greater light" on the firmament and to the waters above the firmament. Is this plan "complicated"? On the contrary, it is clear and simple.

23. 2 Pet. 3, 5: "They willingly are ignorant of, that by the word of God the heavens were of old, and the earth consisting out of the water and by the water." That the world even now is sustained by water *agrees perfectly with modern chemistry.* Only one-fourth of our globe is land, the rest is water. Vapors of water are all around and above us in the atmosphere, and waters are above the

firmament. These waters are vast reservoirs necessary for the maintenance of the universe. This and the so-called Neptunian theory, according to which the solid parts of the earth were formed from aqueous solutions, agrees well with the Scriptures. But how does the Copernican plan together with the so-called Plutonic theory, according to which the earth once was a glowing mass, agree with the Bible? Not in the least. Nor does Newton's idea of an attractive energy, proportional of the particles involved, which operates constantly and uniformly between the atoms of matter, agree with it. Also the modern chemist knows nothing of such attraction or gravitation. The astronomer and physicist who work downward on the basis of Newtonian hypothesis, and the chemist who works upward by deductions based upon experimental facts, do not arrive at a common conception of the properties of matter. The chemical affinities of atoms and molecules, investigated by the chemist, exhibit phenomena of an entirely different order. He finds that each kind of atom and each kind of molecule reveal attractive affinities peculiar to that kind, attracting certain other kinds of atoms or molecules, but not all particles of matter, irrespective of their chemical character, nor yet any in a simple proportion to their weight. Knowledge of the properties of matter gained by experimenters does not agree with the theory of matter required by the Newtonian-Copernican scheme. And indeed we have no need of Newton's fictitious "occult energy of gravitation," for this energy can apparently be rationally accounted for by the operation of forms of energy experimentally known to us, such as electrical and magnetic attraction. We reject therefore the Newtonian "gravitation" so full of amazing contradictions—and resort to an electrical theory in accounting for the attractions of the universe as well as for its repulsions. In making choice between the regent vague and contradictory astronomical conception and the scientific chemical investigations I unhesitatingly take my stand upon the experimental science of the chemist.

24. *The Newtonian-Copernican theory presents difficulties, so far insoluble,* which have accumulated since the days of Laplace, Newton's successor. Discrepancies between observed phenomena and Newtonian theory—for instance the phenomenon of repulsion in place of attraction in the case of the tails of comets when those bodies approach and recede from the sun—present problems which now

at length have produced an undercurrent of skepticism among the theorists themselves. Prof. Henry A. Rowland of Johns Hopkins University takes Newton's law of gravitation (popularly supposed to be the one theory of the scientist which has been infallibly demonstrated if no other has) and shows that, on the contrary, it remains mere hypothesis, unsusceptible of demonstration. He remarks that the so-called "proofs" of Newton's law are all erected from premises in which the law *is assumed without proof,* and therefore do not demonstrate it. "Thus a proof of the law," he says, "from planetary down to terrestrial distances is physically impossible." (In his address as President of the Physical Society of America, delivered October 28, 1899, and printed in the American Journal of Science, for December, 1899.) In nature we find phenomena which can in no wise be referred to Newton's law of gravitation—phenomena due, in fact, to an energy diametrically opposed to such gravitation, being repulsive instead of attractive. Newton's hypothesis that every particle of matter in the universe attracts and is attracted by every other particle has no place in nature, and already a vague unrest is apparent against it and begins to produce an attitude of doubt toward all Copernican-Newtonian theories. Newton himself once said of the gravity idea: "It is to me so great an absurdity, that I believe no man who has in philosophical matters a competent faculty of thinking can ever fall into it." (Newton's third letter to Bently, cited in the Annual Report of the Smithsonian Institution for 1876.) But later Newton embraced that same great absurdity that he had denounced in 1693, in his prime. Thus Newton in his old age lost the competent faculty of thinking in philosophical matters. And what a commentary upon all his devoted followers since, whose faculty of thinking in philosophical matters has been so incompetent that they, too, have fallen into the same great absurdity!

25. *Comets do not comply with the Copernican-Newtonian system.* They have no uniform direction, as the planets have. They as often move in an opposite direction. They never stand still or move backwards like the planets do, but unchangeably keep the same course. The great comet of 1858 was seen 269 days, and was not retrograding or going backwards for a time. But this must needs have been the case, if the Copernican theory were correct. For they claim that the planets are retrograding *because* the earth moves about

the sun. The fact that comets *never* retrograde is, as also Tycho pointed out, an indisputable argument against the Copernican hypothesis. So undeniable is this fact that the theorists have not even tried to refute it. Even their "higher calculation" which so often helped them out, in this case was quite impotent. Baffled by these wanderers of the sky, the Copernican writer Joseph Hamilton exclaims: "The comet cannot belong to our system." (Other Worlds. 1903, p. 104.) But that does not remove the difficulty! — Further, the sun is not the centre of their orbits. Comets do not obey his laws. They are largely independent of his attraction. They rush almost close to the sun, and break away again into space. If ever they come back, it is not in obedience to the sun's attraction. The law of attraction is not universal as Newtonians claim. There is more variety in the universe than their philosophy has dreamed of. The fault with too many scientific men of to-day is that they sometimes generalize too quickly.

26. The Copernican assertion that *the earth, revolving in a year around the sun,* is kept in its course by the force of the sun's attraction, *contradicts* most positively the laws of *gravitation*. According to the Newtonian theory, every molecule of the earth's mass attracts and is attracted by every molecule of the sun's mass. Thus the earth and sun should always present the same faces toward one another, as if a network of taut wires connected all their molecules; for the direction of gravity with each body must be perpendicular to the point from which the gravity of a larger body works upon it. Similarly, the direction of gravity of our earth should be constantly toward the sun, on the supposition that there is an attraction working from that orb upon it. Yet this is not the case, for if the earth moves in an orbit around the sun, the direction of its gravity necessarily must be changing each moment. What power could cause this constant change? The astronomers and philosophers will have some trouble in naming a force so powerful as originally to have inaugurated, and since to have maintained, a revolution of a mass of molecules which must needs continually overcome the gravational pull of each molecule toward the sun. But while the Newtonian theory leaves us in the dark, the Biblical system avoids the difficulty attendant upon a postulate of the translation of the earth through space.

27. *An orbit of the earth around the sun,* together with a rotation on its own axis in twenty-four hours, *is an impossibility.* On June 21st the earth is said to be diametrically opposed to the position it occupies on December 21st, having moved halfway round the sun. Now, the Copernicans say: "Each position of the earth's axis is parallel to all the other three." *As the poles maintain their parallelism*—the south pole pointing to the sun in winter and the north pointing to the sun at midsummer—the effects produced from these causes must be exactly opposite to each other. In other words: a diagram of the reputed orbit of the earth combined with the parallelism of the poles shows the sun almost as far to the north of us in the summer as it is to the south in winter; and that is where we should see it if the theory evolved by the Copernican system were correct. This is the Scylla which the Copernicans cannot avoid. Further, the revolution of the earth is inconsistent with the theory of tangential impulse. If we turn to some Newtonian text-book upon the subject we find, that impulse is supposed to have been given to the earth in the direction of a tangent, in a straight line. They say: "This original impulse was imparted to it when it began its orbital motion." But if this were true, the earth's axis could not be parallel in all four positions. On the contrary, one and the same end would always point away from the sun. But if this were the case (as it must be according to the laws of motion) how will the Copernicans account for the change of seasons? This is the Charybdis which threatens with shipwreck every Copernican theorist. The Biblical system is not at a loss to account for the four seasons. But the Copernicans must contradict a law of nature to account for them. For it is a well-known law that each rotating body which moves from its place receives the direction of its movement from the kind of its rotation, and vice versa, the direction of its rotation from the direction of its movement. If the earth rotates toward the east, it must also move to the east. But while the earth is said to rotate always to the east, from September 22 to June 21 it revolves around the sun in quite varying directions, the combination of the two movements thus becoming utterly absurd! If a body rotates in an eastern direction, it must also move to that direction. And if at the same time another force acts, enforcing another movement, perhaps to the west, then the one of the two forces which is the stronger must

neutralize the other. What would follow in the case of the earth? It always would show the same face to the sun, as the moon does to the earth. It is a remarkable fact that this is also the case of both Mercury and Venus, whose revolution about the sun is a matter of ocular telescopic demonstration.

28. Everyone knows that the laws of Kepler and the hypothesis of Newton, with the mathematical solutions developed by Newton, Lagrange, Laplace, Adams and Leverrier, are all in explanation of the mechanism which would result from a *fixed* sun, holding in equilibrium about himself planets moving in elliptical orbits which practically re-enter themselves with every revolution of the respective planets. But observations which have been carefully registered for many years show that the fixed stars, so-called, seem gradually moving apart in one part of the heavens, while in the opposite part they seem gradually to be coming together. On the Copernican postulate, this indicates *a swift movement of our solar system* toward the part of the heaven where the stars appear to be moving apart. Prof. Newcomb estimates the velocity of this motion at ten miles per second. Mr. Fison thinks it is between twelve and eighteen miles per second ("Recent Advances in Astronomy," London, p. 47.) The orbital velocity assigned to the earth during her annual revolution about the sun, on the Newtonian-Copernican hypothesis of a fixed sun, is about nineteen miles per second. In addition to this motion, and to her daily rotation, we are now to credit her with *a forward velocity through space* which is one-half her orbital velocity, or more. In the case of the moon, this translation through space is to be taken into account, together with the moon's velocity in her own orbit about the earth, and her much greater velocity in moving with the earth in the orbital revolution about the sun. We see at once that by this supposition Kepler's ellipses are completely swept away. It means the complete collapse of nearly all the current estimates of astronomy. And it also means, as Gen. de Peyster has correctly said, "The contradiction of observations." (The Earth Stands Fast, New York, 1900 p. 66.) If the earth not only speeds around the sun in an orbit of about six hundred millions of miles, and with the sun through space at a rate of ten miles per second or more, then really it requires a little care to realize the quandary and perplexity in which the modern astronomer is placed. But does it not seem the height of absurdity to apply

to the mechanism of a system, whose controlling sun is conducting his planetary satellites swiftly through space, the explanations framed for a system whose controlling sun was considerd practically fixed in space, holding his satellites in elliptical orbits, one outside the other, about himself as their common centre? But if the laws of Kepler are quite false, representing appearances but not facts, and if Newton's law is out of the question as applicable to the actual plan of the universe, must we not then reject them? *The Bible plan avoids all those difficulties* arising from a postulate of the translation of the solar system through space, and it renders a rational explanation in the premises. Should not, then, all astronomers accept it and thus restore that confidence in the Bible which they as a class have labored so zealously to destroy?

29. Copernicans say that the moon moves *slower* when nearer to the sun, because then it is more attracted by the sun. But of the earth they say that it moves *faster* when nearer to the sun, because then it is more attracted by the sun. Thus the stronger attraction retards the motion of the moon, but accelerates that of the earth. And to reverse, when the sun is more distant and his attraction less, does the moon move faster, but the earth more slowly? Do you understand it? But Laplace informs us: "Though the results seem to contradict each other, yet they suffice to show that the sun's attraction of earth and moon is the only true cause of these irregularities." That certainly means 'bringing into captivity' our reason. Yet, that sacrifice must be brought, because the theory of Newton must be defended under all circumstances. The above reminds us of a sentence in "Popular Astronomy" (XIII, p. 171): *"The law of attraction and repulsion of matter is the reverse of the theory of Newton."* That Newton's law of gravitation is only approximately correct, has been evidenced from Newton's time to the present. The moon is the only celestial body whose distance can be measured by means of a base line drawn on the earth's surface. Hence if discrepancy between theory and observation is found in the case of the moon, where our observations are the most exact possible, it requires a strong bias in favor of theory to inspire confidence in the apparent harmony between theory and observation in the case of more remote bodies.

30. But the moon does not afford all the discrepancies. The

three celestial bodies, whose respective distances from us make them the most competent, after the moon, to bear witness, namely *Mars, Venus and Mercury*, are the very ones which *also disclose discrepancies*, while our own earth likewise fails to respond to theory in certain respects. Great faith is required of those who in the face of such facts still esteem Newton's formula to be the exact mathematical expression of a great natural force! Prof. Asaph Hall, the well-known American astronomer, also concedes the inability to account for all the observed phenomena on the basis of Newtonian hypothesis. When Laplace died in 1827, it was thought by many that nothing remained to be done. But the passing years have changed all that. We are tempted to apply to Laplace one of his own mottoes: "Time destroys the fictions of opinion, and confirms the decisions of nature." Time, in fact, which tests all things so severely, has shown that *many of the results of theoretical astronomy are erroneous*. For instance, "The major axis of the planet Mercury is moving faster than it ought from the action of the known forces. In this case it is very certain there is no defect in the theory, and we are obliged to search for a force that can produce this motion." (Hall, in Popular Astronomy, May, 1897.)

31. The fact that Newton's law evidently expresses the equations of the solar mechanism with approximate accuracy is the reason given by Prof. Newcomb and most others for still believing that the postulate of universal attraction cannot be *fundamentally false*. But there is an explanation which reconciles every fact in the case. We must remember that *Newton had Kepler's empirical laws before him* —laws deduced from the well-nigh daily observations of Tycho Brahe, which had been carried on with remarkable accuracy through many years, and therefore gave a close approximation to a true mathematical statement of the planetary motions about the sun.

32. The old Ptolemaic system had the *epicyles*, or curves like those made by a point in the rim of a forward running wheel, to explain the retrograde movement of the planets. But Proctor, the greatest Copernican writer of the last century, informs us: "The great astronomer Kepler found in the seemingly capricious motions of the planet Mars the means of abolishing at once and for ever the cycles and epicycles, the centrics and eccentrics, in which astronomers had so long put faith." (Our Place Among Infinities, 1897, p. 186.)

For *Kepler held that the motions of all planets around the sun are ellipses.* But time had its revenge. Soon astronomers taught, as we have seen, that the sun, too, was moving. Herschel gave him a velocity of 20,000 miles an hour. Now astronomers make it over 300 millions of miles in a year. As soon as the sun himself was seen to move in space, those dreamed of ellipses were totally swept away. They were no longer ellipses, but instead a number of long-stretched epicycloids. And "if the *elliptical orbits* be *crushed out of shape by further modern theories,* the underlying and overlying (also ever lying) theory of gravitation must go with them." (Albert Smith, Kepler's Laws of Motion.) The Copernicans were in no small dilemma. For do they not now have the *epicycles* in their own system which so often and so vigorously they had denounced? How must they feel when reading the words of their goliath Proctor that the 'great astronomer' Kepler has 'at once and for ever' *abolished* the epicycles? How did he manage it? Still, in a certain way Kepler was right, namely, in as much as the *earth* does not move in epicycles. And she neither moves in ellipses or any other orbits, to be sure. But have the Copernican writers made it plain to the general public that the earth no longer moves in ellipses? An examination of treatises rather exhibits a studious avoidance of frankness here. Time and again they speak of Kepler as having given us "a proper conception of the solar system and the motions of the planets," and of the laws of Kepler as being "established" (Science History of the Universe, New York, 1909, vol. 1, pp. 76. 78) though they must know that Kepler's 'conception' does not in the least agree with modern research. Why do Copernicans so often and repeatedly use that authoritative language? *They try to hide their own weakness by the claim of authority and infallibility.* Prof. Pearson characterizes this weakness and deficiency in his well-known "Grammar of Science" in the following frank expression: "The obscurity which envelops the principia of science is not only due to an historical evolution marked by the authority of great names, but to the fact that science, as long as it had to carry on a difficult warfare with metaphysics and dogma, like a skillful general *conceived it best to hide its own deficient organization.* There can be small doubt, however, that this deficient organization will not only in time be perceived by the enemy, but that it has already had a very discouraging influence both on scientific recruits and on intelligent laymen. Anything more hopelessly illogical than the statements with regard to force and matter current in elementary text-books of science, it is difficult to imagine."

33. The Copernican theory of *the earth's motion is against the nature of the earth itself,* because the earth is cold and indisposed to motion. Already by Polacco, Tycho, and Dr. Schoepffer and many others this has been pointed out. This argument has also widely been admitted by the Copernicans themselves in the case of the sun, arguing that the sun himself is a dark body with only a photosphere around him. This hypothesis they embraced to strengthen their heliocentric theory. But when by the aid of the spectroscope it was shown that the sun and stars are glowing, gaseous bodies, and when further it became apparent to astronomers that they are moving through space with an enormous velocity, they needs dropped that argument.

34. But while the earth must needs be immovable in virtue of its cold nature, modern scientific investigations have made it clear that *sun and stars are heated, fiery, electrical bodies. It therefore must appear very natural to us that they should move very swiftly.* It is the nature of heat to produce light, chemical action, electricity, magnetism, and mechanical motion.

35. Do you question, how it is possible for the heavenly bodies to fly round the earth in twenty-four hours to compass their daily courses? Is it not hard to conceive a speed so enormous? In our times this objection is without force. *In our days such great velocity is very plausible.* Tell a country lad, in a place where there is yet no railroad, that we can make a mile in one minute, and he will think this utterly impossible. And yet we know that light and electricity travel over 186,000 miles a second. Therefore that argument is rendered void. The celestial bodies having the nature of light and electricity are splendidly fitted to have such swift velocity as to finish their course around the earth in twenty-four hours.—But are not the stars too far away? There is not a vestige of truth in these distances. The entire calculations of the distances and sizes of the stars are reduced to nothing as soon as we look upon the earth as stationary.

36. The earth does not move round the sun each year, since no *parallax or change of position on the starry sky is perceptible.* Already the illustrious Tycho de Brahe, the father of our modern *prac-*

tical astronomy, the 'Prince of Astronomers' as he is called by the celebrated Bessel, urged this argument against the Copernican theory. He said if the earth were speeding north, the stars would go south, and vice versa. But lo, the stars never change their positions. According to the Copernican theory, on December 21 the earth stands 185 millions of miles away from the point where it stood on June 21, while yet a star which you have seen through the telescope culminating on December 21, you will see through the same telescope on June 21 culminating on the same spot of the firmament. When so many millions of miles away, we do not notice anything. Besides the sun, too, is rapidly speeding through space, and the earth again must follow. That increases the rate of our earth's speed to over 100,000 miles per hour. But no changes whatever in the stars above us! We are 5,000 millions of miles away from the place where we were 4,000 years ago, and yet Job saw the stars in the very same places where we see them to-day! Says Prof. Newcomb: "To the oldest Assyrian priests Lyra looked much as it does to us to-day. Among the bright and well-known stars Arcturus has the most rapid apparent motion, yet Job himself would not to-day see that its position had changed." No change of position among the stars! Indeed, the mechanism of the Copernican theory is an incomprehensible absurdity. "No star has yet been found for which this great orbit diameter of 185 millions of miles subtends an angle greater than about one second of arc." (Prof. Harold of Columbia University in The New International Encyclopedia, New York, vol. 2, p. 143f.) For this reason men of intellect like Sir Francis Bacon, Shakespeare, Milton, and a vast cloud of others rejected the Copernican postulate, projected by the imagination. The Copernican astronomers point to the great distances of the stars, because they need such fabulous and inconceivable distances to prop their system. They are a requisite of their doctrine; but they are only a popular delusion and hallucination. They exist only in the brains of Copernican astronomers and of the unthinking folk and become void as soon as we return to the belief in the stability of the earth.

37. In 1675, the Danish astronomer Ole Roemer discoverd that light has not always the same, but a varying velocity, which he measured by *the eclipses of the moons of the planet Jupiter.* At certain times it was observed that these moons became dark. And

after these regularly occurring eclipses were once recorded, it was easy to predict them for any time in the future. This was done. But now it happened that they always were behind the predicted time—sometimes up to sixteen minutes. Only one came regularly at a certain time. To Roemer now came an idea which made every Copernican shout with joy, namely—he pronounced that difference to be due to the annual revolution of the *earth*. Because the earth, he said, is 185 millions of miles farther away after half a year, it takes a longer time for the light to reach us from the Jupiter-moon. The Copernicans are very proud of this argument. But it, too, may be viewed from another side. For *we may assume just as well that the difference is brought about by the epicyclical motion of the planet Jupiter* instead of that of the earth. The epicycles, at regular intervals, bring Jupiter nearer to the earth and again carry him away. Or that difference may have yet other causes. By the way: Roemer used the diameter of the earth's annual orbit for a base-line in his calculation; but as this diameter constantly varies, the result that light travels 186,000 miles in a second, must be also uncertain, even from the Copernican stand-point. If, however, the annual revolution of the earth is an illusion, Ole Roemer's entire calculation falls to the ground. The great Italian astronomer Cassini never admitted it. Fontenelle declared it to be "a seductive error." (Draper, p. 173.)

38. Another Copernican argument faces us. Proctor writes in the British Encyclopedia: "When *Bradley observed the phenomena of aberration,* the evidences of the earth's annual revolution were rendered equally convincing." This is the pet argument of the theoretic astronomers. They feel a thrill of ecstasy when it is mentioned. Prof. Ball calls it "the beautiful phenomenon of the aberration of light." Dr. White calls it "Bradley's exquisite demonstration of the Copernican theory." This wonderful discovery helped the Copernicans out of the rut. Chamber's Encyclopedia even says that Bradley's theory "furnishes *the only direct and conclusive proof we have of the earth's annual motion."* (Article 'Astronomy,' p. 799.) So here we have the 'proof' with which the Copernican system stands and falls. It must therefore be hard for the Copernicans if this—as they themselves admit—only direct and conclusive proof of the earth's annual motion should fall. What, then, is that new

discovery? The thing is this. The English astronomer Bradley, it is claimed, discovered an annual motion of the stars. But because this motion contradicted an annual course of the earth around the sun, he said that we see the stars three months late, as it takes that long for their light to come to us. Thence the word 'aberration.' Notice, that also this supposition is based on the Copernican dream of an enormous distance of the stars! For were it not so, then *the observation of Bradley proves the contrary and is a strong argument against the Copernican system,* yea entirely overthrows it in case the assertion in Chamber's Encyclopedia is correct that it is their only direct and conclusive proof. But since the inconceivable distances are but absurd assumptions and conjectures, must not a theory built upon these premises be a ridiculous guesswork and fallacy built upon a foundation of sand? As Dr. Woodhouse, a late professor of astronomy at Cambridge, England, confessed: "We are here compelled to admit the astounding truth that, if our *premises* be disputed and our facts challenged, the whole range of astronomy does not contain the proof of its own accuracy." (Earth Review, January, 1893.) But besides this, what can force us to accept for this phenomenon as the only possible explanation a movement of the *earth* under the stars? May there not be other causes for that motion, for instance a motion of the stars themselves, caused by that great electrical body, the sun, or who knows by what other causes? For there are more things in the world than our human philosophy imagines.— But Bradley continued his observations and found—yet another circular motion of the stars which takes place in a little over eighteen years. This was attributed to a rotation or motion of the earth's axis. But why again must the *earth* be it? May not that motion— if really it does exist—be caused by something else, say by an electrical vortex among the stars, or by the sun's spiral movement from north to south, and again backward, or by many other causes yet unknown to us? And such assumption is taken for a proof, yea the only direct and conclusive proof for the earth's annual motion? How, then, can they say, that Bradley's theory is an "exquisite demonstration of the Copernican theory"? Does not that Copernican theory thus appear to be a hoax and a swindle just as much as that ancient mythical speculation brought from India to Europe by Pythagoras (hundreds of years before Christ), which Copernicus revived? The heathenish philosopher Niketas of Syracuse, and Aristarch of Samos (who was born 267 before Christ), likewise entertained the Copernican view.

39. *Another striking testimony in favor of the Biblical plan is given by the spectroscope,* which indicates incandescent (white or glowing with heat) metals as the chief constituents of the stars. This is precisely what our present knowledge of electricity would lead us to expect. Carbon is perhaps the most economical conductor of high resistance. The incandescent electric lights of commerce are obtained by raising to a white heat a thin strip of carbon arranged between the poles of a voltaic battery which generates a strong current. Carbon poles are used in the production of the arc-light. This is a striking analogy of the stars. This explains to us why the stars disclose no disks when observed through the telescope. On this basis of a grand electrical plant we can also account in a rational way for the extinction of the light of some stars, to reappear again in a short period—a fact which on the basis of the current Copernican theory (according to which the stars are very large bodies) cannot be explained, a fact which induced the Copernican Prof. Langley to exclaim, "It is surely an amazing fact that suns as large or larger than our sun should seem to dwindle almost to extinction, and regain their light within a few days or even hours; yet the fact has long been known, while the cause has remained a mystery!" (The New Astronomy, 1880, p. 227.) But while the Copernican astronomer stands before this fact amazed and perplexed as before a mystery, it is, on the other hand, very plain according to the Biblical view and modern science. For according to these the stars may be only at a relative short distance from us and yet fully serve their purpose. With the analogy of the incandescent electric light before us, we can dismiss the immense sizes and distances which the Copernican hypothesis compels us to assign to the stars.

40. The most rational astronomical plan is that which embraces the observed relations most comprehensively and explains them most simply, on the basis of the mechanics of nature known to us on the earth, requiring the least amount of inventions. *The Biblical plan, explained on the electro-magnetic basis, has a remarkable advantage over the other in point of simplicity and ability to explain more of the phenomena in the universe.* William B. Taylor (Annual Re-

port of the Smithsonian Institution for 1876) demonstrates that not an iota of progress has been made in two centuries toward an explanation of gravitation as a kinetic force. To conceive of gravitation as an *active* force lands us in all sorts of contradictions. But to think of work being done by a *passive* force is perhaps even more ridiculous. Hence Mr. Taylor declares that all that is left to us is to conceive of an "occult" force of universal attraction! In other words, this devoted disciple of Newton, in his treatise on gravitation, comes to the conclusion that all devout Copernicans must dethrone their reason and must accept an "occult" force which repels when it should most powerfully attract, and attracts when it is most free to fly apart. This is the conclusion of what is probably the most profound and comprehensive investigation of this problem ever undertaken. But while gravitation cannot even account for the relations between the members of the solar system, and for the phenomena of falling bodies, electro-magnetism not only accounts for both, but enables us to recognize that the same force which holds the orbs together supplies light, heat, actinic energy, and electrical energy throughout the system. We must prefer these *known* forces which are known to produce both attractive and repulsive phenomena, together with the Biblical system, which is demonstrable on this basis without dethroning the human reason in the process. The Biblical plan has a great advantage in simplicity and credibility in virtue of explaining the entire physical universe as one closely-related and orderly system; whereas the Copernican hypothesis represents the solar system as isolated, in independence of the rest of the physical universe, with the suggestion of many other independent systems. For this reason the esteemed astronomer Bandes has well said of the Biblical system: "It has more truth in itself—nay, the different phenomena may be demonstrated very easily with it."

41. The moment we are forced to conclude that the most minute variations of climatic and other conditions on the earth are results of the radiation from sun, moon, planets, and stars, that moment it becomes most rational to assign to these bodies a function of special service to the earth such as the first chapter of the Bible teaches. *The special office of the sun, moon, and stars is to minister to the earth.* These celestial bodies were ordained to divide between the day and the night, for signs, and for seasons, and for days and

for years, and to be for light-bearers in the firmament or expanse of the heavens to give light "on the earth." Again we have the very definite statement that God set them in the expanse of the heavens, "to give light on the earth," and to rule during the day and during the night, and to divide between the light and the darkness. (Genesis 1, 14-18.) It is the view of the entire Holy Writ that the earth is the central body of the universe, that it stands fast, and that sun, moon, and stars are but ministering to it. And is this astronomical scheme of Scripture crude and primitive? So one would imagine from the cheap learning everywhere abounding which sweeps the Bible aside, with a magnificent flourish of intellectual superiority over Christian faith, on the ground that its fallibility is fully exposed in its astronomy! But what is the fact? All practical astronomers are compelled to admit that the system implied in Scripture accounts for all the observed phenomena more competently than does the Copernican hypothesis. Even the late Prof. Proctor, who was perhaps the most dogmatic champion of Newtonian-Copernican orthodoxy among astronomers of standing, as well as the most virulent in applying it to discredit the Bible, wrote in the Encycl. Britannica (vol. 2, p. 777): "All the observed movements, and all the peculiarities of the observed relations were fully explained by this system," meaning the system of Tycho Brahe which is essentially that of the Bible.

42. *Scripture speaks of the phenomenal appearance of the daily revolution of the sun and stars in a way which implies the reality of their daily motion about the earth.* Psalm 19, 1-6: "The heavens declare the glory of God; and the firmament sheweth his handiwork. Day unto day uttereth speech, and night unto night sheweth knowledge. There is no speech nor language, where their voice is not heard. Their direction is gone out through all the earth, and their words to the end of the world. In them hath he set a tabernacle for the *sun, which is as a bridegroom* coming out of his chamber, and rejoiceth *as a strong man to run a race.* His going forth is from the end of the heaven, and his circuit unto the ends of it: and there is nothing hid from the heat thereof." The psalmist here speaks of the swift motion of the sun. That this is a typical speech pointing to Christ and to the quick extension of his kingdom, is expressly stated in the New Testament Rom. 10, 18. Christ is here in the nineteenth

psalm compared to the sun. And which is the point of comparison? The swift *motion* of the sun. The meaning is: as the sun moves around the whole earth with a remarkable speed, thus also Christ, the Sun of Righteousness, runs a speedy race bringing to all inhabitants of the earth the joyful tidings: "God so loved the world, that he gave his only begotten Son, that whosoever believeth in him should not perish, but have everlasting life." (John 3, 16.) "His word runneth very swiftly." (Psalm 147, 15.) But now we must carefully note that *the point of comparison in the Old Testament types is always taken from the reality*. Thus the saving of the eight souls by water was a type of the saving of souls in baptism. The slaying of the lamb was a type of the suffering and death of Christ. The looking at the serpent of brass that was put upon a pole, was a type of the faithful looking upon the crucified Christ as the only Savior. The high priest Aaron was a type of the great High Priest, Jesus the Son of God. We see that the point of comparison is never something only imagined, but is always taken from the reality of things. The object-lesson to be taught by the type is always found in a real fact. Just so here. The point of comparison is the fact that the sun runs so swiftly. Thus Christ runs very swiftly with the gospel of our salvation to all the inhabitants of the earth. The Bible here treats the phenomenal, or apparent, movement of the sun as the actual movement of that body. In all instances of Scriptural references to the heavenly bodies or the earth, as physical types of moral truths, the object-lesson is ever found in the phenomenal appearance of things, Scripture citing the phenomenal appearance as the physical fact. *All* Biblical references to astronomical facts are undeviatingly consistent in implying a certain astronomical system and no other. Any person left to gather his astronomical ideas from the Bible alone would necessarily imbibe a belief in this particular scheme.

43. Psalm 74, 16 we read: "The day is thine, the night also is thine." And which is the natural cause of day and night? Is it caused by the rotation of the earth on its axis in twenty-four hours? This passage has no reference to that Copernican hypothesis. Asaph, who wrote this psalm inspired by the Holy Ghost, believed that day and night are caused by the daily revolution of the heavenly bodies, for he says, *"The day is thine, the night also is thine: thou hast prepared the light and the sun."* Ponder the wording! Should not the

remarkable contrast in this sentence induce all believers in the Bible to earnest thinking and research before accepting some contrary philosophy? Luther remarks: "The sun causes daytime not so much in virtue of his splendor and light as in virtue of *his motion* by which he moves from east to west rising again after twenty-four hours and making another day." (Erl. lat. I, 56.) Another such remarkable contrast we find Ecclesiastes 1, 4. 5, where Solomon, the wisest of all men, says: "The *earth* stands forever; but the sun ariseth, and the *sun* goeth down, and hasteth to his place where he arose." These words are clear and unmistakable. Is it possible to harmonize this plain Bible statement with the Copernican assumptions, that the earth is flying around the sun at an enormous rate, causing the surface of the earth to move a thousand miles an hour at the equator, in order to give us day and night? Every candid person must admit the impossibility of harmonizing the teaching of the Bible with the teaching of the Copernicans. What should be done in such a case? Call for facts. *The Bible, the evidence of our senses, and all known facts declare that the sun moves, thus causing day and night, summer and winter.* The Bible, the evidence of our senses, and all known facts also declare that the earth is at rest and "stands forever." Can the Copernicans gainsay or deny this? Listen to the honest and noble confession of Dr. Woodhouse, the well-informed professor of Cambridge University, England: "When we consider that the advocates of the earth's stationary position can account for and explain the celestial phenomena as accurately, to their own thinking, as we can to ours, in addition to which they have the *evidence of the senses, and Scripture and facts* in their favor, *which we have not*, it is not without a show of reason that they maintain the superiority of their system. Whereas, we must be content, at present, to *take for granted* the truth of the hypothesis of the earth's motion, for one thing. We shall never, indeed, arrive at a time when we shall be able to pronounce it absolutely proved to be true. The nature of the subject excludes such a possibility. . . We are *compelled to admit* the astounding truth that, *if our premises be disputed, and our facts challenged, the whole range of astronomy does not contain the proof of its own accuracy!* Startling as this announcement may appear, it is nevertheless true." (The Earth Magazine, London, No. 65, p. 9.) This frank admission from a distinguished Copernican astronomer should be noted. And I could here cite a score of scientists whose names are known the world over, who admit that for Newton's law and the Copernican hypothesis they have no proof worth mentioning. We have the evidence of our senses, and Scripture and facts in our favor, which they have not.

44. *The Bible is the infallible truth also in natural things, therefore also these must be accepted as important and significant.* Dr. Stoeckhardt is correct in saying: "In fact, *there are no insignificant, small, things in Scripture* which were of no importance to faith. We often hear it said that the Bible is no text-book for the natural sciences, history of the world, geography, etc., but a book which teaches religion and tells about God and divine things. That is correct. But from it never follows that the natural, historical, and geographical references in the Bible may not be looked at as competent and altogether trustworthy; no, everything in the Bible, also the natural, historical, and geographical references have, even because the Bible is a religious book, a relation to God, Christ, faith and life of the Christians. *Everything in the Bible—also what seems to be trivial, small, and unimportant—is profitable to us for doctrine."* (In an article "The Bible the Infallible Word of God," Lutheraner, 1892, No. 20.)

45. *The Bible never speaks according to the erroneous conceptions of men.* When the Copernicans were confronted by the authority of Scripture which declares that the sun moves and the earth stands fast, they answered, Scripture speaks according to the erroneous conception of the people. But this opinion is false and a blasphemy against God, who is the divine author of the Bible. If the Bible would err in secular and earthly matters, how could it be our guide in matters eternal and spiritual? Says Prof. L. W. Dorn: *"It is absolutely impossible that a passage of Scripture should intend or endorse false conceptions.* The doctrine of the Lord is perfect, says the psalmist. Thy word is truth, says our Lord and Master Christ himself. What God has inspired, that is correct, that is true, may it concern the way of salvation in a restricted sense, or other things which the Lord has spoken as truth in the Scriptures. *What God speaks through the holy men, always complies with the facts, the real condition.* If, therefore, it should be the case that that, which we perceive with our senses, or which we know by our reason, were

contrary to the Word of God, we must not follow our senses and our reason, but trust in the Scriptures that they are right. God is omniscient; he knows all things. In nature, in history, in all branches of human knowledge he is acquainted with everything a thousand times better than the wisest of men on earth. God cannot err. Our eyes may deceive us, our ears may deceive us, all our senses may deceive us. The reason of the wise and learned on earth often wanders on peculiar and wrong roads, but *God's Word never deceives us. The true, correct, meaning of a Bible-word never leads us to false, erroneous, conceptions.* The Bible is always right in all things. It tells the truth about all things of which it records something, for its words are words of the Holy Ghost." (Syn. Report, Tex., 1910, p. 68f.) The Christian who takes Scripture as an infallible guide, is able to take forth the precious from the vile, and to detect unchristian hypotheses and deductions. The necessity for some such touchstone is great in our days.

46. *The intended meaning of the Holy Ghost is but one—the literal sense.* "The real and original meaning of any passage is the one which the Holy Ghost intended and which is given by the original meaning of the words themselves." (J. Gerhard, de interpret., §133.) "The literal sense of every passage is only one. Were there more literal meanings of a passage, the Holy Scriptures would be altogether dark; for to mean not one only, is equal to mean nothing certain. What is spoken in a manifold sense, is ambiguous. But to say this of Holy Scripture, is wrong." (Aug. Pfeiffer, Thesaur. hermen., cap. III, p. 140.) True, many words of the astronomers are uncertain and erroneous. But *"we* have a more sure word." 2 Pet. 1, 19. "Thy word is a lamp unto my feet, and a light unto my path." Psalm 119, 105. "The statutes of the Lord are right, rejoicing the heart: the commandment of the Lord is pure, enlightening the eyes. The fear of the Lord is clean, enduring forever: the judgments of the Lord are truth and righteous altogether." Psalm 19, 8. 9. — Dr. Graebner: "Nor is the meaning of those words a variable quantity. The signification of these signs was determined when the signs were given by inspiration of God, and while these signs are what they are, *the signification is the same to-day* and will be the same forever. Of two or more different interpretations all may be wrong, but *one only can be right,* and what the text is

thereby understood to say is true, being what God would have us know and hold, because thus *saith* the Lord." (Fundamentals of Interpretation, Quarterly, 1897, p. 434.) "The literal sense of one and the same passage is only one. For in every language and in every kind of speech it is a custom that the author intends to indicate only one meaning by the same words which stand in one and the same context, unless he (the author) speaks with the intention to deceive." (Baier, Comp. II, §43.)—*"Holy Scripture cannot have a manifold meaning, or it is ambiguous.* Only a deceiver ascribes to Holy Scripture a manifold meaning. God's Word has only one meaning, although the things otherwise can signify a thousand different things. The Reformed Church claims that the words 'eat' and 'drink' in the Lord's Supper have a twofold meaning. They mean: we receive only bread and wine, and again: we receive the body and blood of Christ in a spiritual way. The Papists have invented a fourfold meaning, and the modern theologians claim Scripture to have a manifold sense. But there is no comfort in this for a Christian, as he must always be in doubt which is the intended meaning of the Holy Ghost. . . It is not in the power of man to decide if a passage is to be understood in the real, literal sense, or not. *We must not deviate from the literal sense of a word or sentence, unless Scripture itself urges us to do so."* (Syn. Report, North, 1867, p. 40. 43.)

47. The Bible must be explained by itself. *We must accept the words of the Bible as they stand there in their plain, real, literal meaning, unless the Bible itself makes it necessary to deviate from that meaning.* Such necessity would be if the verbal meaning were against the context or against other passages of Holy Writ. No necessity to leave the plain meaning would be if one urges the human reason and common sense or the sole possibility. As from the probability of a thing never rightly can be concluded its reality, thus it is wrong to say that we must leave the plain, real, meaning of the words because they may have a figurative meaning. Luther: "I have often said that he who will study the Holy Scriptures, must take great care to accept with all diligence the plain words and never deviate therefrom, *unless he be urged by an article of faith* to understand the words otherwise than they read. Because God speaks, it does not behoove you frivolously to turn his word as you will, unless necessity urges you to understand a text otherwise than the words

read, namely, when faith does not allow such meaning as the words give." (Sermon on Genesis.) We insult the Holy Ghost, the divine author of the Bible, if we carry into it the explanations and thoughts of our own human reason or the so-called facts of Copernican philosophy. Only he is lead by the Holy Ghost and honors God who accepts the plain speech and words of the Holy Ghost. Prof. R. Lange: "Never are the divine sayings by divine weakness and frailty, as it were, mixed with any error which human sagacity and human wisdom must remove, as if man were to correct a divine mistake. Everything which is carried into the words of God by a human explanation, intended to correct and improve the same, actually *changes* the divine word and *the divine meaning* which is implied in that divine form. *Such change tears down the divine character and the divine origin of the word; it abolishes God's Word and puts man's word in its place.*" (Lehre und Wehre, Foreword, 1880.) The Bible is very able to explain itself. There is no clearer book on earth. The best human book as compared with the Bible is only like a candle light before the glorious rays of the sun. How, then, is it possible that some find in Scripture a different meaning than the plain words involve? Answer: these are plain words and passages, indeed, but passages and words "which they that are unlearned and unstable *wrest* (twist, by inserting a false meaning), as they do also the other Scriptures, unto their own destruction." 2 Pet. 3. 16. "Whoever has grammar in the highest meaning for himself and no other clear Scripture against himself, he has the correct understanding of a passage on his side." (Prof. E. Pardieck, Lehre und Wehre, 1914, p. 344.)—"We must unwaveringly adhere to the *words* of Scripture as they, certainly in their context, stand there and read, even if the whole world, our own self included, should talk against it. Therefore, Luther at Marburg wrote the words *This is my body* with chalk before himself on the table. As soon as we drop the verbal meaning of Scripture, thinking we must do away with 'contradictions,' we are lost and put our own opinion, or the opinion of our party, in place of the Scriptures." (Dr. F. Pieper, Ibid., p. 254.)—The only safe course is to have a simple faith in God's Word. It is the Word of God, of which it still holds good that heaven and earth shall pass away, but that God's Word shall not pass away. God's Word is as firm and immovable as God Himself. Oh, the foolish Christian who bases his faith upon the fallible human reason! Nor should the foundation of our faith be reason in some places and God's Word in other places, nor God's Word squared with the corrupt reason of man, but His Word alone and always, in its plain, simple, and definite statements. This ought to be the position of every true Christian.

48. *When Scripture speaks according to the external appearance, or in a figurative sense, this becomes clear by the context or other passages.* Thus the phantom or apparition before King Saul (1 Samuel 28) is distinctly called Samuel, because Samuel was wanted, and Samuel it was supposed to be, and Samuel it *appeared* to be. But that it was not Samuel, Scripture itself indicates; for we read 1 Chron. 10, 13. 14: "So Saul died for his transgression which he committed against the Lord, even against the word of the Lord, which he kept not, and also for asking counsel of one that had a familiar spirit (literally: asking counsel of a familiar spirit—a Python) to enquire of it; and enquired not of the Lord: therefore he slew him, and turned the kingdom unto David, the son of Jesse." Under the name of conversing with the dead, Saul held intercourse with Satan—and not with God through Samuel. For the latter, Saul would never have been slain, nor would Samuel ever be called a familiar spirit, a demon.—Also the passage Joel 2, 31: "The sun shall be turned into darkness, and the moon into blood, before the great and the terrible day of the Lord come." This turning into blood is called a *wonder* (Hebrew *mophet*) in verse 30: "And I will show wonders in the heavens and in the earth, blood" etc. The very same expression 'wonder' is used where it is said of the waters of the River Nile that they were turned to blood. And in both places, too, the 'turning into' blood is called in the original text: *haphach.* (Exodus 7, 9. 20.) Does not this clearly show that in *both* places a real 'wonder' is meant? How, then, can it be said by some that the prophet Joel speaks only *'optice'*—according to the external appearance? How can there arise any difficulty if we accept the literal, real, meaning as the text, context and other passages give it? Also the learned Dr. Pocock accepted this passage in the literal sense and held that "before the last judgment there will be *wonders indeed* in heaven and earth, the dissolution of both without a metaphor."—Further, when it is said Psalm 2, 8 that "the utter-

most parts of the earth" are given to Christ for his possession, and Psalm 22, 27 that "all the ends of the world" shall turn unto him, we clearly see it must be a figurative speech, as Scripture itself indicates that Christ has redeemed the *people* for his possession and that *these* shall be converted unto him. Thus we see that by the expression "ends of the world" a great multitude of people is meant.—Or, when we are told in Revelation 7, 1 of "the four corners of the earth," we see from the connection of these with the four winds, and from the information that someone is 'holding' them, namely, the four winds, that it must be a figurative speech. The four cardinal points are meant. The verse reads: "And after these things I saw four angels on the four corners of the earth, holding the four winds of the earth, that the wind should not blow on the earth, nor on the sea, nor on any tree."—A similar passage is Job 38, 13: "That it might take hold of the ends (wings) of the earth, that the wicked might be shaken out of it." By the expression 'shake out,' Scripture indicates that the word 'ends' must be taken in a figurative sense.— But when in the Sacrament the Lord says: "This is my body," "this cup is the new testament in my blood," we nowhere in the whole Bible find a hint that this also is unreal or figurative speech. The same must be said of the many passages which speak of the earth as resting and of the heavenly bodies as moving. Nowhere in the whole Bible we find any contrary passages or anything which could indicate a figurative sense, or hint to a different meaning, of those passages. We truly can say of all those many passages: "This is the plain meaning, which also is in keeping with other passages of Scripture." (Apol. of the Augsburg Confession, 159.) "What do the foolish people expect? Do they think that *Scripture repeats the same thing in clear words so often* without due reason? Do they think that the Holy Ghost does not express his word with certainty and carefulness, or does not know what he says?" (Ibid., Article of Justification.) Must we not, therefore, take all those passages in the literal, or real, sense? Were it possible that God meant the *contrary* to what the words indicate? Then, who could trust him any longer in *any* of his words? Thus, for instance, when the Holy Ghost Joshua 10, 13 says: "The *sun* stood still," did he mean: "The *earth* stood still"? To interpret Scripture this way is blaspheming the Holy Spirit of God, who is the Spirit of truth and conviction, and who *never* deceives us. Rightly our fathers have said: "By such interpretation (of the Joshua passage) *a dangerous rule of exegesis* is established which may make all Scripture uncertain." (Syn. Report, East, 1868, p. 18.) And why should we not accept the literal meaning of those passages? Because of the Copernicans? Let Dr. Walther answer. He says: "It has been shown that the gentlemen admitted in clear words that they absolutely have no evidence and no certainty for their system, that they themselves do not believe in it and only demand of the uninitiated faith in their *infallibility."* (Lutheraner 29, p. 103.) Shall we not rather ascribe such infallibility to Scripture? Here you have a touchstone whereby you can test your position regarding the doctrine of inspiration, which is one of the most vital questions in the Lutheran Church. All Scripture contains the view that the earth has a central position in the universe and that the heavenly bodies (created later) are only ministering to it. Must you not accept this testimony of your God? Is it not dangerous, indeed, to let the trustworthiness of your Bible depend on the shifting views of human science? "For we know *in part*, and we prophesy in part. But when that which is *perfect* is come, then that which is in part shall be done away." 1 Cor. 13, 9. 10.

49. Luther: "They should know that *one word of God is all*, and all are one." If the Bible is *false in one*, it is *false in all*. This is a just and logical saying. "If the Bible errs in astronomy, geology, physics, chronology, etc., then you can also in theological questions believe in it only so far as you have from other sources convinced yourself of the correctness of its statements." (Prof. Bente, L. & W., 1904, p. 87.) If the Copernican system is correct, then Genesis is a myth. Is Scripture which has enlightened the world for thousands of years now to be eclipsed by a science which has erred so often and is altogether fallacious in so many things? Much, indeed, is at stake. Satan is bold. A false principle of an immense import is practiced, namely: *"They falsify Scripture* by totally ignoring words that do not suit them, or *by discarding the right and obvious meaning and sense and by inserting a different meaning."* (Dr. Stoeckhardt, L. & W., 1905, p. 8.) Let us be true philosophers and not blindly follow the teachings of either old or modern astronomers and their many wild assumptions—but let us ever *follow the truth!* The conjectures of the astronomers of to-day are, for the most part,

preposterous conceptions which read very much like stories from Laputa—conceptions which do not lie in front nor behind the telescope or spectroscope, which are neither written in the starry sky nor anywhere on earth, but which can only be found in Dream-land. "There is no steadfastness in their mouth." Psalm 5, 9. However, "let every man *be fully assured* in his own mind." Rom. 14, 5. *We must be fully persuaded and convinced.* Will the dreams and assumptions of modern astronomers give us that conviction? Of Kepler's laws of motion the American author, Edgar Allan Poe, said: "These vital laws Kepler *guessed*—that is to say, he *imagined* them." (Cameo Edition, 1904, vol. IX, p. 19.) Will Kepler's 'imagined' so-called 'laws' make us *fully assured?* Indeed, not! That can give us little comfort and assurance. *"A Christian conscience cannot come to rest before it is in full harmony with the Scriptures in everything* it believes—believes for the reason that Scripture says so. The sooner the rag of speculation tears from the garment, the better. It may otherwise become very dangerous in the hour of death. The devil may whisper to me: What is right for *one* clear word of Scripture, is right as well for the other. Have you treated a clear passage from Scripture as if it did not exist for you in Scripture, how is it, that you trust in words like: The blood of Jesus Christ, the Son of God, cleanseth us from all sin?" (Dr. F. Pieper, L. & W., 1905, p. 16.) Luther: "Nothing is more blessed than conviction, and nothing is more wretched and nearer to hell than uncertainty." (7 Cal. 26.) "Good consciences cry after truth and the right instruction from the Word of God, and to them death is not so bitter, than bitter it is to them to be in *doubt* about something." (Apol. of Augsb. Conf.) Let us, then, not be *wavering*. "For he that wavereth is like a wave of the sea driven with the wind and tossed." James 1, 6. Let none of us teach, hold fast, advocate or defend the Copernican system with a wavering conscience not fully assured.— May the following testimony prompt our assurance. The Bible Explanation of Dr. Wilischen, 1742, comments on Joshua 10, 13: "We can *impossibly* explain and understand these words differently without open injury to the divine truth. The Holy Ghost narrates such miracle in two verses with the same Hebrew words. How should we expect this Spirit of Truth, who guides us into all truth (John 16, 13), to speak otherwise than he means? *How should we believe that he puts his speech according to the false conception of the common people?* If we admit this error which is greatly unfavorable to the divine honor and the essential veracity of God, it will be said of many more other passages of Scripture that the Holy Ghost only speaks according to the feeble conception of men and their foolish opinion, but not according to the essence and real being of a thing. Here we urge not so much *the antiquity of this opinion* (though in Holy Writ it was taught and confirmed long enough), namely, that the whole large globe of the world with land and water stands immovable according to the arrangement and preservation of its all-wise Creator; the sun and moon, however, have their prescribed orbits, real rising and setting. The system of Copernicans has as many difficulties as that of the ancient Ptolemy and that of Tycho de Brahe which here cannot be shown at length. Enough! We adhere to the clear words of Holy Writ, urge also other *plain passages which otherwise from the Copernican stand-point must, in fact, be very much abused and explained against the meaning of the Holy Ghost.* Against this may our dear Lord Jesus, who is the Truth Himself (John 14, 6), protect us!"—Bettex spoke well, when he said: "The Magna Charta of a Christian is *the Word of God explained by itself.*" And likewise the illustrious Lutheran dogmatician John Gerhard, who said: "They *dishonor* the Word of God by saying that it accommodates itself to the human opinions." "In a word *there is no sufficient certainty but of Scripture only* for any considering man to build upon. This, therefore, and this only, I have reason to believe; this I will profess; according to this I will live; and for this, if there be occasion, I will not only willingly, but even gladly lose my life, though I should be sorry that Christians should take it from me. Propose me anything out of this Book, and require whether I believe it or no, and seem it never so incomprehensible to human reason, I will subscribe it with hand and heart, as knowing *no demonstration can be stronger than this: God hath said so, therefore it is true.*"—Works of Wm. Chillingworth, M. A., Oxford University Press, 1838, Vol. II, pages 410. 411.

50. *By the Copernican system credulity and superstition are enthroned and unbelief and infidelity invited and encouraged.* The well-known Dr. Valentine Ernest Loescher said: "No sooner was the very uncertain doctrine brought up that the sun is at rest and

our globe revolves around him, than the contempt of Holy Writ and infidelity notably increased. On the other hand, vanity was rampant, and the desire to accept and circulate absurd opinions." (His Life, by Engelhardt, 1856, p. 283.) The celebrated Dr. Walther wrote: "As is well known, the modern astronomers or star-gazers claim that by the Copernican system (according to which the earth moves round the sun) the Bible—according to which the sun moves round the earth—is completely refuted and overthrown. And yet these gentlemen demand that the Christians now should believe just as much in the Copernican system as before they did in the Bible. For they say that he who is no professional astronomer, has no right to judge their teaching; and therefore it were a great shame that yet there are people who, though not experts in astronomy like themselves, do not believe everything they say. By these *edicts and bulls of the would-be infallible astronomical popes* the worldlings, indeed, are now generally frightened; not to come under the ban of the star-gazers, and to be recognized as enlightened they, in *blind credulity,* repeat everything that those 'infallible' popes tell them. They patiently admit that they understand nothing about astronomy, and therefore cannot judge in this question; but if they want to be counted for wise, they must close their eyes and have a strong faith. But with the Christians it is different. However strong their faith may be in the word of their God, they are very slow in accepting opinions of men. Here they must be convinced by indisputable arguments, or they will not believe." (Luth. 1873, p. 103.) Astronomy has driven God from heaven—such is the last word of modern rationalism, such the latest utterance of that science that has arrayed itself against the Bible. "Copernicus, Kepler, Galileo, Descartes, and Newton came—and when their work was done the old theological conception of the universe was gone. These five men had given a new divine revelation to the world." (Dr. Andrew White, Warfare, I, 15.) *"The New Astronomy* came—and the Bible and the church as *infallible oracles* had to go, for they had taught that regarding the universe which was now shown to be untrue in every particular." (Lucifer, Dec. 23, 1887.)—So the real question is not one of astronomy, but of God, faith, and salvation. "The foundations are destroyed." Psalm 11, 3. True, there are many Copernicans who do not embrace the extreme Copernicanism with its arrogant unbelief; but also with them this is a question of the greatest importance, *because the authority of Scripture is at stake* even with them. This was clearly seen by Prof. Lindemann, Sen., of the Teacher's College at Addison, Ill., and therefore he emphasized it in the beginning of his booklet against the Copernican system, saying: "Because the truth of Holy Scripture is at stake, therefore the above question is to me of paramount importance." Already Luther has clearly seen it. But he was not frightened by the Goliath of modern astronomy. When he heard of Copernicus who died three years before him, Luther said: "That fool would turn the whole art of astronomy. But, as Holy Writ indicates, Joshua told the sun to stand still, and not the earth." (Erl. 62, 319.) And again he says: "The Word of God must not be mocked. I am caught, cannot come out; the text is too powerful. Therefore I say: clean and clear, believe all or believe nothing!" So near to the four-hundreth anniversary of Reformation-Day, let it be our motto: Back to Luther! Let us take him for our model also in this question concerning Copernicus. Luther called him a fool. And must not the same be said of the Copernicans of to-day? "Professing themselves to be wise, they became fools." Rom. 1, 22. Must not every Christian—like Luther—reject Copernicanism on scriptural grounds? We have seen, not one proof can be brought to uphold the Copernican system. But must we not *mainly* reject it, because it is against the Bible? It is, indeed, the solemn duty of every Christian to do so; for, what are we profited, if we defend the *walls* of the Church, but leave the *gate* wide open, through which the whole modern anti-biblical topsy-turvy error with all its superstition, vanity, unbelief, and boastfulness crept in! So let us leave the Copernican tomfoolery, and be it our battle-cry: Back to Luther! Was not that learned Altorfian professor right who said: "The nearer to Luther, the better theologian"? He certainly was. So,

> *"Back to Luther!"* I am calling
> To the stragglers of the herd.
> *Follow*, or you will be falling—
> Deviating from *the Word*.
> Build the prophet's tomb by giving attention
> To his word without restrain;
> *Hold to Scripture* with a firm apprehension—
> Thus will *Luther's fame* remain.

IN CONCLUSION.

Right or wrong, some adhere to that which is popularly taught under the sanction of high-sounding titles; and though they may proudly reject *revelation,* they seem to suppose that 'science' is infallible! This attitude shuts out all calm and earnest investigation for *truth,* and leaves the mind a prey to the delusions of a cleverly concocted scheme.

Many *know* that there is no proof for the Copernican hypothesis, but they are blinded by the cry: "It is accepted throughout the civilized world!" (Dr. Carl Pierson, "The Grammar of Science," 1892.) The most common objection raised against the Biblical system is the *general agreement of the learned.* But voices must be weighed, not counted.

Goethe, the most wonderful intellect of the nineteenth century, says: "Be it as it may, it must be laid down that I curse the accursed lumber-room of this modern conception, and certainly some young, ingenious man will arise who has the courage to oppose this universal, crazy nonsense. The repeated assurance which all natural philosophers have had in this same conviction is the most outrageous thing you can hear. He, however, who knows men, knows how this happens. Good, able, keen brains make up such an opinion on the basis of probability; they assemble proselytes and disciples; such a mass gains literary power; one magnifies the opinion, exaggerates it, and carries it out with a certain passionate excitement; hundreds and hundreds of well-thinking normal men, who are active in other branches and also wish to see lively working in their surroundings, honored and respected—what can they do better and wiser than to give these ample scope, and to consent to what is not their business? And this is then called *general agreement of scholars!"*

The following words of Alfred Russel Wallace (a champion of modern astronomy) are worthy of being remembered: "Official advocacy, whether in medicine, law or science, is never to be accepted till *the other side* of the case has been heard." (Man's Place in the Universe.)

And which is the result that "the other side" has found after a conscientious investigation of the pending documents? Which is the result? Here it is:

"Our result is: the Copernican system is not at all proven. All exertions of science cannot make *the Biblical view* of the relation between the bodies of the universe in the least doubtful; on the contrary, what has been found, only helps to confirm the fact that *Scripture is the truth also in such questions,* and that also *there* it never accommodates itself to the erroneous conceptions of men." (Lehre und Wehre, St. Louis, 1898, p. 334.)

If the above reasons enable even a single soul to throw off the shackles of mere superstitious reverence for the Copernican dogma, and of blind subserviency to a scientific priestcraft which abuses its authority most shamefully, the consequence for good may be incalculable. Released from the humiliating despotic thralldom, our soul can soar up and sing: "The proud waters had gone over our soul. Blessed be the Lord, who hath not given us as a prey to their teeth. Our soul is escaped as a bird out of the snare of the fowlers: the snare is broken, and we are escaped." Psalm 124.

BY THE SAME AUTHOR.

BIBEL UND ASTRONOMIE.

Proof that not a single one of about sixty verses, in which the earth is said to stand still, and the sun and all stars are said to move, may be interpreted in such a way, as if really the reverse were the case. In German. 410 pages, 8°, 1906. Good muslin binding. About twenty illustrations. $1.00 postpaid. Order from: Rev. F. E. Pasche, Morris, Minn.

"**Der Bekenner**": The author stands on a strictly Anti-Copernican standpoint. Undoubtedly he has searched and worked diligently, and his expositions are interesting and convincing.

"**Rundschau**": Pres. A. F. Breihan has favorably recommended this book in a foreword.

"**Kirchenbote fuer Australien**": We bring this nicely appareled book to your notice with the firm conviction that by its publication a great, highly to be appreciated, service has been rendered to all. The author is well known among us as a devoted student of Scripture and natural history by his book "Christliche Weltanschauung." (I have no more copies of this first book. Author.) The contents of this new book are very rich, and every part is interesting and fascinating. The whole has a genuine Lutheran character. We wish for the book the widest circulation.

"**Haus und Land**": We admire the arduous diligence of Rev. Pasche. The book contains a whole library. Whoever is interested in the subject—and who should **not** be interested in it—can very likely find in no library of America an equally fascinating, copious, and instructive work on this theme which must highly interest every thinking man.

"**Lutherische Botschafter**," Oakland, Cal.: Two extremely interesting books! However, the author does not intend to bring something new and interesting, but to emphasize that we Christians can and should keenly believe in the clear words of Holy Writ even then, when it speaks certain things about the origin of the world or about astronomy—the movements of the heavenly bodies, and their relations toward each other, in the orbits which God has prescribed for them. To enable the reader to defeat the philosophers with their own weapons, who contradict Holy Writ by proclaiming their own opinions in cosmogony and astronomy as truth, the author furnishes him with numerous citations from the writings of these men, and at the same time shows how unscriptural, foolish, and untenable their propositions are. By the attentive reading of these books our faith in the verbal inspiration of Holy Writ cannot fail to be strengthened—our faith, founded on the Word of God which says: "**All** scripture is given by inspiration of God." "And the scripture **cannot be broken.**" "**Which things also** we speak, not in the words which man's wisdom teacheth, but which **the Holy Ghost teacheth.**"—We, therefore, recommend to our readers (also especially to our young people in their societies) the reading of these books. To make a wide circulation possible for both books, the author offers them at a very reasonable price.

"**Immanuels-Bote,**" Grand Rapids, Mich.: Perhaps also some of our dear congregation members have been attracted by the "Illustrated Lectures" in astronomy as also by some articles in the papers. Now, such inconceivable fables may be quite interesting for the pleasure-seeking children of this world, but a Christian must be painfully touched by seeing his dear Bible publicly and boldly struck in the face, and the God of Israel defied. Now a booklet has been published which bravely encounters this scoffing goliath of modern science, and battles him successfully with his own weapons, and especially with the sword of the Spirit, which is the word of God. This booklet is: Bibel und Astronomie.

CPSIA information can be obtained
at www.ICGtesting.com
Printed in the USA
LVHW090224191020
669140LV00008B/505